Whitney Museum of American Art	September 27 - November 7, 1961
Norton Gallery and School of Art, West Palm Beach	February 1 - February 28, 1962
The Minneapolis Institute of Arts	March 22 - May 7, 1962
Marion Koogler McNay Art Institute, San Antonio	May 28 - July 31, 1962

by John I. H. Baur

BERNARD REDER

EXHIBITION AND CATALOGUE BY THE
Whitney Museum of American Art

Research by Rosalind Irvine *Curator, Whitney Museum of American Art*

BOOKS THAT MATTER *Published in the United States of America in 1961 by* FREDERICK A. PRAEGER, INC., *Publishers. 64 University Place, New York 3, N.Y.*

Library of Congress catalogue card number 61-17285
Designed by Peter Oldenburg
Printed in the United States of America

FOREWORD AND ACKNOWLEDGMENTS

THIS MONOGRAPH is published on the occasion of the large retrospective exhibition of Bernard Reder's work, held at the Whitney Museum of American Art in the fall of 1961. It contains a catalogue of the exhibition and reproduces virtually everything shown, as well as several other important pieces.

We are most grateful to the artist for his patient cooperation with every aspect of this project. Many hours were spent on interviews, the majority of them recorded on tape by Mrs. Michael H. Irving. Quotations in the following text are from these recordings or from the artist's notes and letters, unless otherwise indicated. World House Galleries, which have represented Reder since 1958, were also most helpful.

Neither the exhibition nor this publication would have been possible without the interest of The Ford Foundation in Bernard Reder, who was awarded a grant in the Foundation Program for Visual Artists in 1959.

While Bernard Reder is primarily a sculptor, he has also designed a number of highly imaginative architectural projects. Several of these have been translated into models and structural drawings by Synergetics, Inc., using Buckminster Fuller's system of construction. I would like to express our gratitude to James W. Fitzgibbon and C. David Sides, Jr., of that firm for their effective cooperation.

Reder's sculpture is conceived in the round; there is no front or back to his pieces and no preferred views. In order to demonstrate the importance of approaching his work from all sides and from various elevations, a double ramp was constructed in one of the Museum's galleries to carry the spectator around the sculpture at different heights. It was designed by the artist, in collaboration with the architect, I. M. Pei, and was built by Robert Catino. Uris Buildings Corporation supervised every phase of this project, which was partially financed by a generous grant from the Uris Brothers Foundation, Inc. We are deeply indebted to B. H. Friedman of the above firm for his understanding help, as well as to all the others involved.

The majority of the illustrations were made from photographs by Charles Uht, the rest from photographs by Oliver Baker, Lee Boltin, Hertz Grosbard, O. E. Nelson, Adolph Studly.

The preparation of this monograph was greatly aided by four people. Mrs. Bernard Reder devoted months to translating foreign articles and reviews, assembling catalogues of past exhibitions, clippings and periodicals, transcribing her husband's notes, providing lists and measurements of his work and helping in many other ways.

John Rewald's earlier monograph (*Bernard Reder*, Florence, 1957) was extremely useful, particularly in his recollections of Reder's years in Paris, on which I have drawn for a long quotation. Miss Rosalind Irvine, the Associate Curator of the Whitney Museum, compiled the chronology, bibliography and index and did much of the research on which this account is based. Mrs. Patricia Westlake, of the Museum's staff, prepared the catalogue and handled many other details in connection with the exhibition and this publication. To all of the above I would like to express my personal thanks.

Finally, the Museum's warmest gratitude is extended to the many private collectors and museums who so generously lent their works to the exhibition and permitted them to be reproduced in these pages. They are: Mr. and Mrs. Walter Bareiss, New York; Mr. and Mrs. Rudolph J. Boyko, New York; Mr. and Mrs. Phillip A. Bruno, New York; Mr. and Mrs. Jacob Hacken, Queens Village, N. Y.; Dr. Morton Hecht, Jr., Great Neck, N. Y.; Joseph H. Hirshhorn Collection, New York; Mr. and Mrs. R. Sturgis Ingersoll, Penllyn, Pa.; Mr. and Mrs. Michael H. Irving, New Canaan, Conn.; Mr. and Mrs. Joseph D. Isaacson, New York; Jay C. Leff, Uniontown, Pa.; Mrs. Vera G. List, New York; Mrs. Gertrud A. Mellon, New York; Mr. and Mrs. John Rewald, New York; Mr. and Mrs. Raphael H. Rhodes, Jamaica Estates, N. Y.; Mr. and Mrs. Seymour J. Rubin, Washington, D. C.; Dr. and Mrs. Louis R. Wasserman, New York; William P. Wood, Haverford, Pa.

ON SCULPTURE

THE HUMAN BEING is born genuinely volumetric-minded. He naturally approaches and enjoys objects volumetrically. Frontal education destroys this natural gift.

Sculpture evolved in the past under the limiting spatial conditions of unvolumetric ages, almost never opposing them.

A new spatial concept has finally begun to evolve in our time. It will enable man to approach earth and everything on it from every point. Man will then find visual evidence of the unhidden truth in the volumetricality of things and thoughts.

Opposed to this is the reigning frontal spirit. Its method is to use the facade to express the contrary of what is behind it, not letting the object speak honestly of its own value. Macchiavelli raises this condition to a negative ethical necessity. It is a mystification of daily human life, creating most of its complications.

Objects in nature are volumetric, all-sided; therefore axiomatic, not theoretical. All views of volumetric sculpture and all approaches to it — from around, above, below — are of the same importance. They have the axiomatic value of the sphere and require no theoretical explanations. In the volumetric approach to sculpture, none of its views can escape the control of the sculptor, the observance of the spectator.

Control can only function if observation is volumetric and not limited to the horizontal line of the floor. In this way sculpture is raised to the status of a true volume.

The method offers to coming generations of sculptors the VOLU-METRIC MOTIF.

ON ARCHITECTURE

MINIMUM WEIGHT in a building puts a roof over the head; excessive weight puts a roof on the head. The weight of a building has an important influence on the mind and spirit of its occupants and of those who pass in the street. Lightness in a building creates an atmosphere in which man may grow freely and with fewer complexes.

The human spirit naturally seeks horizontality and accepts verticality only in proportion to it. A return to horizontal architecture would banish the overcrowding created by monumental vertical buildings. Lightness of weight and structural simplicity would then be possible, and these are the virtues we find in the huts of those peoples who are not so much primitive as less complicated.

Scientific research in the development of synthetic building materials of light weight should be augmented for the benefit of mankind. Architecture must express its love for the individual, not the masses, for only the single human being can be reached by love. This is an ethical goal for architecture in our time.

by Bernard Reder

"... for the statue that is true sculpture must have eight views, and all must be equally good. Thus it happens that the sculptor who is less devoted to this art is satisfied with one beautiful view, at most with two. And by avoiding the trouble of taking something away from this beautiful aspect to make it harmonize with the other six, which are not so beautiful, his statue is badly neglected, and not one out of ten people will praise it if he observes it not only from the side first presented but from all other sides as well. That was where Michelangelo's excellence was apparent, in that he understood the true value of this art and demonstrated its greatness on a higher level."

Letter of Benvenuto Cellini to Benedetto Varchi, June 28, 1546 (from Hermann Uhde-Bernays, ed., *Kunstlerbriefe über Kunst*, Dresden, 1926, p. 99).

Wherever Bernard Reder has lived and through whatever tribulations an adverse fate has led him, his passion to create and his unshakeable dedication to a morality totally comprised by art have sustained him. In Czernowitz, Prague, Paris, Havana, New York; among the villainous tombstone cutters of Bukovina and Bessarabia, in flight from the Gestapo or imprisoned in Spain, Reder has never stopped working, never compromised, seldom ceased to trust in miracles. And they have come, if only in the nick of time. "Without any one of them," he says, "we would not be alive today."

Reder's absolute assurance of mission is reflected in the absolute certainty with which he works. There is no waiting for inspiration, no periods of doubt or hesitation. Art flows from him with a spontaneity which is matched by his astonishing inventiveness and freshness of concept. Some of his latest bronzes, six feet or more in height and complex in form, were created at the foundry, directly in wax, within the span of a few weeks; for many an artist they would be the respectable output of a year. During those unhappy times when he was deprived of stone or plaster, a profusion of drawings and woodcuts poured forth. Hanging in the studio today is a sketch of a horse on a paper napkin, done on a train crowded with refugees during World War I; the long series of woodcuts illustrating Rabelais was executed while he was in hiding during the German occupation of France. At other times his creative energy has turned to architecture, to city planning, to the design of ocean liners, theaters, museums, even a device for preventing accidents in the bathtub.

Yet there can be no doubt that Reder is, above everything, a sculptor. (A friend once remarked that he looked like one of his own carvings — round, massive, compact, with short fingers and powerful hands that seem made to hold a mallet and chisel.) It was as a stone carver that he began, and it was from the block that he derived the paramount principle of his art. This he calls "volumetricity," the functioning of forms in the round — no frontality, no dominant views, but an organization equally meaningful from every angle and every elevation. The sphere (in which the block can be inscribed) is thus the ideal volume, unchanging from every side. To Reder this is more than an aesthetic credo. It is a principle of life and a touchstone of morality. It is the embodiment of coherence, from which any departure is a step toward chaos. By projection it is the harmony of love and the meaning of religion.

This passionate feeling for a self-sustained order, essentially classical in its nature, underlies all Reder's work to a greater extent than may at first be apparent. It is easy to recognize in his early carvings with their dense clusters of rounded forms, but the bronzes done after 1950 inaugurate a quite different style — baroque, open, alive with broken surfaces, rich in fantasy. Yet in these, too, an underlying discipline becomes felt. No movement is dissipated in space. Despite their complexity, the forms turn in upon each other, closing circles, completing volumes. It is as if the block had been opened in ways impossible to stone, but also as if its spirit of self-sufficiency had miraculously been preserved. Paradoxically, Reder has built an open and transparent baroque art on classical principles, and this unconscious dichotomy, this instinctive balancing of opposites is an important factor in creating the tension, the variety and the strength of his mature work.

Another factor is certainly Reder's imagination, which has produced so rich an iconography of strange birds and beasts, hybrid musical instruments, exotic costumes and inexplicable confrontations. At first it found its outlet only in the drawings and woodcuts. But it was too strong a force to be banished for long from his sculpture, and in the late bronzes it has reached a degree of fantasy equal to that of his graphic work. Many of the odd devices which one finds here spring from purely formal needs; if a harp is too flat it can be given a second wing and thus be developed into a spreading V-shape to complete the design in depth. But there is no doubt that Reder takes a pleasure in these mutations which could not be satisfied by abstract or formal means alone. "Why should one abstract?" he says. "Every form is in nature, completely clear and unbroken. Why have you to break things in pieces to serve art?"

The nature to which he turns in his sculpture is not, however, to be found in common experience. It comes from an inner life which has been nourished by his background, by his reading and by the play of his imagination. His subjects are drawn sometimes from books — principally the Bible and Rabelais; sometimes from legend — Amazons, centaurs, minotaurs and the like. But these are a minority. By far the greater number are born in his own mind from sources too deep to discover: a flowering cat, a multibranched telescope, a huntress with her captive antelope, a woman bearing a house of cards, a nude holding a sphere over a pyramid. Or he may recall a childhood episode when he was required to write a paper on the good Samaritan and made up a story of a man who lifted a horse into a tree so that it could eat the fruit which was out of its reach. This, too, has become sculpture.

One cannot overestimate the influence of Czernowitz, where Reder was born 64 years ago, on this intense life of the imagination. "I am asked from time to time to explain the motives of my work, their meanings, whether they are symbols and so forth," he said recently in a speech at the Museum of Modern Art. "I can only answer that these motives spring from the imaginative influence of my early surroundings. . . . It was simply a town, this my native town, sheltering up to 70,000 inhabitants, depending on how many were left after the persecutions. Most of them walked in their individual ways, driven by Hasidic enthusiasm, by longing to help mankind as a whole or individuals, motivated by other convictions, but always impelled by pure enthusiasm. Their walk is slightly dancing, abrupt running or other curious movements fitting their character, all of them with burning eyes looking while running to heaven or far beyond the horizon, no matter if it was the hasid or the lawyer or I, the only artist in town, or even the butcher Mordche Walter, or the tinsmith Perlmutter. There was scarcely an action in any part of the town which was based on realistic calculation but only imaginative going ahead with results which were even so, efficient, because this magically creative spirit produced an atmosphere of harmony."

Now Chernovtsy in the Russian Ukraine, Czernowitz was then part of the Austrian empire. Nearby was the town of Sadagura, an important center of Hasidism. This religious movement had been founded in the 18th century by Israel ben Elieser, known as the Baal Shem Tow (owner of the good name). Born in the Carpathian mountains not far from Czernowitz, he had taught a joyous piety in which nature was the intermediary between man and God. Human love, openly proclaimed, was part of his basic ethic, and a sense of kinship with all mankind. A villain, he said, is only your own reflection; look into his face and it is a mirror in which you see yourself. Reder's earliest memories are strongly colored by the Hasidic atmosphere of his birthplace. His father recited the Psalms by heart. At the court of the local rabbi, where Reder was taken as a child, he once saw an old man climb on a table, cradling a Torah in his arms as if it were a baby, and dance with such joy that he begged for wine to become sober. There, too, he heard the story of the rabbi who left his pupils for twenty-four hours once a year to go, it was said, to

1. Two Nudes. 1933

Pencil. 4⅛ x 9⅞.
World House Galleries.

heaven. But a sceptic among his students hid at the appointed time under the rabbi's bed and watched until early dawn when he saw the rabbi rise, put on peasant clothes, tie a cord around his waist, pick up an axe and leave the house. The pupil followed him to a hovel in the forest where the rabbi cut down a tree, chopped it up, bound the pieces with his cord and, taking them to the house, made a fire for the old woman who lived there. Running back to the court, the student told the others that the legend was not quite true: he had seen the rabbi go maybe higher than heaven.

Not all the Jews of Czernowitz were Hasidim, but even among the others religious legends flourished. These appear to have been of folk origin, embroidered by the imagination of the people on the text of the Bible. They were stories of Lilith, the first woman; of Adam's death at the age of 930 years and his ascent to heaven in a chariot of light drawn by four eagles; of the sun and moon joining him at the gates, black-visaged as Ethiopians because they could not shine in the face of the Father of Light; of the captivity in Egypt and how the Jewish mothers hid their children in the mountains and fed them at night until the Egyptians barricaded the road, whereupon the rocks grew breasts and suckled the children. They were the refuge of an oppressed people, a flight into a shining and legendary world. The quality of Reder's own imagination is close to them, and he has read the four volumes of Louis Ginsberg's *The Legends of the Jews* nearly as often as *Gargantua and Pantagruel*.

2. Bird Bride. 1951.

Woodcut. 26¾ x 20¾.
World House Galleries.

When Reder was born, on June 29, 1897, his father owned an inn for peasants. At home the family spoke Yiddish. For four years Reder went to a Hebrew religious school, then to the Austrian schools, conducted in German. Today he speaks six languages with surprising, if unorthodox, fluency, but as a child he had difficulty with any subject not primarily visual. The only exception was literature, and even here his early attitude toward words was evidence of his sculptural bent. "When a word leaves your mouth," he says, "it is immediately an object which you put on the table that those who wish can examine it from every side. It has no narrative quality; it is a material object, a volumetric image." He left the lyceum for good in 1914, when he was drafted into the Austrian army, and served throughout World War I, hating all of it. He was stranded in Serbia in 1918; it took him three months to walk home.

Early in 1919 Reder decided to be an artist. He still remembers with gratitude his father's response, even though the latter had little comprehension of what art meant: "You do well, my son, it is a fine thing." With a sheaf of drawings and watercolors, he went to Vienna and showed them to a professor at the Academy. Discouraged by a chilly reception, he continued to Prague, where he hoped to obtain a French visa that would permit him to study in Paris. When this, too, failed, he enrolled at Prague's Academy of Fine Arts. For about a year he concentrated on drawing and print making, studying with Peter Bromse and working in life class with such concentration that he has never felt the need of a model since.

It was at six o'clock one morning (an hour when many of Reder's most momentous decisions have been made) that he decided to become a sculptor. Making some drawings of sculptural projects, he took them on the same day to Jan Stursa at the Academy and told him he wanted to work in stone. Stursa refused but suggested he do two works in plaster and bring them back to him. Reder had no tools and no materials, but he told his story to the owner of a plaster workshop who gave him clay, a corner to work in, and even cast his two pieces in plaster for him. On the strength of these, he was admitted to Stursa's class where he continued to model in clay and plaster for about a year and a half, learning much but still frustrated in his desire to carve.

Late in 1922 Reder returned to Czernowitz where he supported himself for the next seven years by making monuments for cemeteries in order to work independently at his own art. He also fell in love with Gusti Korn, whom he had known before he went to Prague, and in one of his notable six-o'clock-in-the-morning decisions he resolved to marry her.

"I could not wait. I got dressed and ran to the flower shop, but of course it was not open at that hour. I had to wait outside until eight o'clock. I had no money, but when I told them why I wanted the flowers they gave me credit. So I filled my arms. I took as many as I could carry. I looked like a walking flower market. I thought my mission was too sacred to take a streetcar, so I walked down the hill and all the way to her house. When I got there she was still asleep, but her sister came to the door. I told her to give the flowers to Gusti and tell her I loved her. I felt very shy at that minute and went away as fast as I could." They were married in 1924.

During these years Reder was working in every spare moment at his art. Even before their marriage he had found a big block of stone in the village where his father was born and had brought it, in a cart

3. Witch and Owl. 1951.

Woodcut. 27½ x 21.
World House Galleries.

drawn by four horses, to a field behind his future wife's house. This was on the outskirts of Czernowitz, and the field was bordered by railroad tracks and a station where trains for the Polish border stopped. As a result, Reder often had a curious audience while he carved his stone into a massive figure called *Birth*, to the accompaniment of audible remarks that it looked more like a monster than a woman.

Slightly later, Reder's parents-in-law built him a studio in the same field, a low thatched building like the peasant houses of the surrounding countryside. Here he carved a *Prodigal Son*, a *Harmonica Player*, a *Double Torso*, a study of interlocking crystal shapes in wood to show the interpenetration of forms, and some fifteen to twenty other works, most of them now destroyed or lost. Several were given away; none was sold. Eventually half of the studio had to be rented as a cowshed to a neighboring farmer, and while the cows and the sculpture shared it harmoniously enough (the stones taking on a rich patina in the process), there was no longer room for the sculptor. So, for a time, Reder returned to drawings, woodcuts and watercolors. His subjects were biblical — some from the Old Testament, some from the Apocalypse — and also purely imaginary. He made up, for instance, the story of an unfinished torso and bust, which escaped from a sculptor's studio and had many strange adventures wandering across the world. He illustrated it with a series of woodcuts that appear to have verged on the surrealist. These, too, have gone, which is a pity since they were his first mature works to evolve from the inner life of fantasy that was later to play so important a role in his art.

In 1927 Reder boldly entered an international architectural competition for a structure to house the monument to Columbus at Santo Domingo (now Ciudad Trujillo in the Dominican Republic). His design was a dome, and with characteristic thoroughness he made several models, and nearly ninety technical drawings of its construction. While he did not win the competition, he was encouraged by the award of a prize. The following year he went to Prague for several months, taking with him a group of his watercolors which he gave to numerous friends and collectors. After his departure, one of the latter — a woman — assembled enough of them to hold a surprise exhibition at the Rudolphinum, Reder's first one-man show, which he never saw.

In Czernowitz the atmosphere was darkening. After the war it had been ceded to Rumania, and anti-semitic demonstrations, unknown during Austrian rule, became frequent. The workshop of Reder's brother-in-law was closed by persecution. Once Reder was attacked by a man with a revolver; once he rescued his father-in-law from an assailant. There was increasing friction with the non-Jewish tombstone cutters. They had Reder's license revoked; briefly it was restored, then taken away again. Unable to work at his sculpture or his trade and without means of support, only one path seemed open. In 1930, the Reders left Czernowitz forever and returned to Prague.

There they rented a vacant storage room in a factory on the outskirts of the city. In the factory's courtyard was an abandoned pavilion which had been used for a fair, and this became Reder's studio. With the last of his savings he bought stones from a nearby quarry, the hard red and gray sandstone of the region. He began to work as he had never been able to work before, all day and every day. And he began to sell an occasional piece to a few private collectors who came to the studio. Unlike Czernowitz, Prague was an international art center where much modern French work could be seen. Vincent Kramâr, whose collection included cubist canvases by Braque and Picasso, did much to encourage local artists, including Reder. A big exhibition of French sculpture opened in Prague soon after Reder arrived; there he first saw the work of Maillol, who was later to become one of his most valued friends.

It was during these seven years in Prague that Reder established his mature style. From the beginning, a feeling for ample volumes was manifest; massive spherical and cylindrical forms which echo each other with variations, play against each other in ponderous counterpoints, balance each other from every view and angle in the three-dimensional orchestration of the whole. His dominant theme was the female nude, and his drawings of the period look a little like those of Renoir. But no strong contemporary influence is apparent in the sculpture. Perhaps he was closest in spirit to Maillol, at least in the classical harmony of his forms, but where Maillol was sensuous, Reder was nearly abstract, and where Maillol was a modeler, Reder was a carver — and therein lay a great difference. The stone itself, the three-dimensional block with its weight, its density, its fullness of volume, played a vitally important role in the creation of these works. To Reder it has always been an immoral act to cut stone into the gestures and naturalistic textures of a Bernini, say. The block makes other demands — for unity, for containment, for that quality he calls volumetricity. In this he was closer to Michelangelo than to Maillol. "The tragedy of Michelangelo's private life may have been caused by his broken nose," Reder says today, "but as an artist his eternal dissatisfaction was embodied in a revolt against the spirit of the Renaissance — frontality — which he was forced to obey by those who commissioned his work, whereas his sculptural spirit was the block. All his blocks with forced frontality are so constructed that, had he not been stopped by the Renaissance's niches and room corners, etc., they would have been continued in the round and have resulted in closed volumes. That is clear in those blocks which he executed without frontal limitations, such as the *Pietá* in the Duomo at Florence or the *Crouching Boy* in the Hermitage. Michelangelo's unique stature as the first block-minded sculptor has been neglected from his lifetime to our days."

Reder's own *Bather, I* (fig. 31), the major surviving work of his Prague period, has this same fulness of volume, this formal unity. The subject is relatively unimportant. The face, for instance, is barely indicated; it plays a lesser role than the sphere of the hair, which echoes the spheres of the breasts and breaks the long cylinder of the torso. Every form is countered and balanced. They turn in upon themselves, rotating majestically about the very center of the block, formally meaningful from every aspect and almost (if not quite) devoid of sensual connotations. Several torsos of the same years (fig. 28) are less complex in organization but equally compact, self-contained; Reder has emphasized their relation to the block by leaving its top surface untouched, as flat as it came from the quarry. None of the above works is polished, nor is there much variation in texture or other surface ornament; the stone is stone and the forms are volumes.

While Reder was primarily interested in carving during his seven years at Prague, he did not entirely neglect other forms of art. Several small bronzes were produced, such as the *Bather* of 1934 (fig.

30) and the *Two Seated Women* of 1934 (fig. 32). These modeled pieces, though remarkably monumental for their size, have a more sensuous quality than the stones; like his figure drawings of the period, they suggest the fullbodied grace and physical vitality of Renoir's nudes. At the same time he was experimenting with architecture and particularly with a concept that has fascinated him throughout his life — an exhibition building for sculpture embodying the "volumetric" principles on which his own work is based. This project has gone through many stages, culminating in his "honeycomb" building of the 1950's. In Prague he had a different idea, which can still be studied in a number of drawings; a circular structure several stories high in which the permanently installed sculpture took the form of caryatids supporting the floors and placed at regular interval around the perimeter of the circle. The center of the building was open, forming a circular well in which other sculpture could be placed and thus be seen from all sides and from the different elevations of the various stories. In a further development of this idea, the floors were to be transparent so that the caryatids also could be viewed from several elevations. In America, many years later, he constructed a large-scale model of such a building.

In 1934 the Reders took a six-month trip through Italy, Spain and France, spending several days with Maillol at Banyuls. Soon after their return, Emil Filla called at the studio to see Reder's sculpture. Filla was a cubist painter and president of Mánes, an association which included some of the leading artists of Prague and which had its own gallery. He offered Reder a one-man exhibition there, although Reder was considerably younger than most artists whom the association had so honored. The show, held in 1935, included 38 pieces of sculpture, a few in wood and bronze but the great majority in stone. Although little was sold, it was unquestionably a critical success. Jaromir Pecirka wrote a review for *Prager Presse* (given first as a speech at the opening) which is still one of the most perceptive appraisals of Reder's work in stone. For he understood how the artist's forms were "developed from the block and organized by the strictest law of proportion applied from all sides and all viewpoints," and although he suggested a sequence of influences from archaic Greek to Maillol, he concluded that Reder had "succeeded in separating Millol's principle of form-harmony from its sensuous implications and . . . transposed it to the boundary of the abstract." Shorter reviews, universally favorable, appeared in at least a dozen other papers and periodicals, including some of Vienna, Basel and Paris.

Two years later Reder fulfilled an ambition of his youth. Urged by Maillol and encouraged by his exhibition, he moved to Paris, intending to settle there permanently. The four years that followed were to be fraught with hardship and danger, but at first it seemed as if he had reached a true haven. Wishing to be near Maillol, he rented a small villa at Le Vesinet, outside the city, where a pleasant garden afforded space for his sculpture and an outdoor studio. There he went on with his carving, taking little part in the artistic life of Paris and meeting few of its artists — sufficient, as he has always been, to himself and his work. Soon after his arrival, the critic and art historian, John Rewald, called on him. Rewald's impression of the villa was still vivid when he wrote his excellent monograph on Reder some seventeen years later.

"Its garden was abundantly peopled with large and small sculp-

4. Woman, Cock and Clock. 1951.

Woodcut. 28 x 22.
World House Galleries.

tures among which appeared a man still young in aspect; his torso bare, his arms powerful and muscled, and his face lit by a smile in which was reflected his joy of living, his naiveté, his sense of humour, and his strength. Slowly I walked around the garden, troubled and yet attracted by the figures in stone and metal which were placed on the grass, either standing beneath the trees or crouching in the shadow of a wall. All of them were enormous women. Their movements seemed to follow geometrical patterns and were contained in square blocks which they filled almost completely with the roundness of their tremendous forms. I became conscious of a strange kind of heavy and colossal beauty which shone forth from these nude bodies."

On September 1, 1939, Hitler invaded Poland and two days later France and Britain declared war on Germany. In the panic of that moment the Reders fled Paris and went to stay with friends at Le Puy in the Haute Loire. Then tension eased (it was the time of the "phoney" war), and early in 1940 they returned to Le Vesinet. Maillol, who had been deeply impressed by Reder's work, spoke to the Wildenstein Gallery about it, and Assia Rubenstein called at the studio. From this came an invitation to join a large group exhibition of contemporary Czechoslovakian art which the gallery was plan-

5. Amazons with Horses. 1952.

Woodcut. 21 x 27.
World House Galleries.

ning. Reder accepted, and the sixteen pieces by which he was represented became a kind of one-man show imbedded in the larger one. About the same time he wrote a pamphlet entitled *The Pointing Machine — The Anti-Christ of Sculpture* in which he re-affirmed his faith in direct carving.

Reder's sculpture in the Wildenstein exhibition included work from Prague and several new pieces, such as the *Torso* (fig. 33) now in the Museum of Modern Art, which he had done at Le Vesinet. These later works did not differ greatly from the earlier carvings.

They were a little less geometrical perhaps, more fluid in form, but they were still female nudes of magnificent amplitude, and they were still nearly abstract creations which seemed to have evolved from the center of the block and to compose in heavy rhythms, equally valid from all sides, around its core. They won Reder a new recognition and brought him a warm letter from Maillol: "I am very happy to observe that people in Paris begin to talk of your great art. I am delighted. You know well that I am in accord with your ideas and your impressive sculpture. I am sure that in America, where greatness is loved, you will be received with open arms. . . . I wish you the great success you deserve for your knowledge and extraordinary courage."

The letter is dated May 19, 1940. Belgium had been invaded, and time was plainly running out. The sculpture from the exhibition was hastily stored in a warehouse, where it miraculously survived the occupation. The sculpture at Le Vesinet did not. It was smashed into fragments by the Germans, for there was no time to move it, no place to hide it. The Reders, themselves, escaped just ahead of the invasion, carrying only a few belongings and Reder's beloved copy of Rabelais. On the train, crowded with refugees, Reder drew on scraps of paper to keep their spirits up; the horse on the paper napkin was done then. Returning to Le Puy, they stayed for a time with an architect named Verdier, then with other friends. Twice the police came for them — Reder heard that they were registered to be sent to Poland — but once they hid and once they were away. Through the tense days of waiting Reder turned to woodcuts and produced no fewer than 52, illustrating Rabelais's *Gargantua and Pantagruel* — to him the highest expression of a joyful life. He also did a series on the Apocalypse.

From Banyuls, Maillol did what he could. On November 10, he wrote Alfred H. Barr, Jr., at the Museum of Modern Art: "I am recommending to you one of my friends, a sculptor of great talent who had prepared large cases of sculpture to bring to New York for an exhibition. He has been prevented by events, but he would like to pursue his project, and to succeed he needs a letter from you to obtain a visa to come to America. Could you ask for it? I can guarantee his excellent spirit and his very great talent, which would certainly have a great success in New York. If you could do this for him you would give me great pleasure." A few months later he was able to notify Reder that a United States visa would be granted.

In Reder's mind the events of the next few months are a blurred dream and their sequence far from clear. The visa never arrived and their efforts to obtain it at the consulate in Lyons failed. Sometime during the summer they joined the stream of refugees flowing into Marseilles, where the American Quaker, Varian Fry, representing the Emergency Rescue Committee, was daily risking his life smuggling liberal politicians, writers, musicians and artists out of the country. They met Fry, which was fortunate since both he and his organization, known in France as the *Centre Américain de Secours*, were soon to play a vital role in their own survival. From Marseilles, the Reders cabled a friend in Havana to ask if he could get them a Cuban visa. They were more fortunate than many. In ten days it was granted, and for a moment the road seemed clear. They returned to Le Puy at night and stayed there in hiding just long enough to pack up their belongings. Then they made their way to the Spanish border at Can Franc, but they had hardly crossed it when they were arrested for illegal transit and taken to a jail in Madrid. Mrs. Reder wrote to the American Embassy and to Fry, but then she and her husband were separated and taken to different prisons — they went through four in all — and for three weeks they had no news of each other and no knowledge of what their fate would be. At the end of that time they were released and warned to leave Spain in twenty-four hours. They took the first train for Lisbon, followed (although they did not know it until later) by two members of the *Secours* to make sure they crossed the frontier safely. They arrived on the same day that Varian Fry reached Lisbon on his way home. The Vichy government had made it impossible for him to continue his work, and fewer refugees escaped thereafter.

The Reders sailed from Lisbon and arrived in Havana early in the fall of 1941. There they applied at once for a United States visa, but it was nearly a year and a half before they obtained it. During this time they lived with a friend, whose underground garage Reder converted into a studio. Here he carved one stone sculpture, *Two Fighting Women*, did several works in plaster, many drawings and woodcuts, and about six paintings in tempera on cardboard. The last are, in some ways, his most interesting Cuban works. They are extremely complex and active scenes involving many figures of nude women, running, standing, sitting, lying, riding horseback and in a variety of other poses. Several of the compositions were drawn from Giotto's frescoes at Padua (one, for instance, from the *Rising of Christ from the Tomb*), but the figures have all been transformed into female nudes, which gives the paintings a strangely ambiguous look. They seem to mark a turning point in Reder's artistic development: a waning interest in the simple monumentality of his early sculpture, a need for the greater challenges posed by multiple figures and more dynamic relations of form. In this respect they forecast the extraordinary things which Reder was to do with stone a few years later.

Despite his makeshift studio and his anxiety to reach New York, life in Havana was not unpleasant. He met several artists, while a group of younger men made an informal circle around him, although they were not his pupils. (He has never wished to teach, and has never taught.) Two one-man exhibitions of his work were held toward the end of his stay — one of woodcuts at the University of Havana, one of sculpture, woodcuts and drawings at the Lyceum Gallery. The local reviewers made much of him ("one of the greatest European sculptors") and regretted that Cuba was only temporarily his home. He might have been tempted to stay were it not for the golden dream of New York.

Early in 1943 their visa arrived, and on February 23 the Reders flew to Miami, took a train to New York and settled themselves in the Benjamin Franklin Hotel on Broadway. Here they stayed for several weeks while Reder worked on drawings and trusted in another "miracle." It came, just in time, in the form of a fellowship, which enabled them to buy a small house in Forest Hills, Long Island, where the garage again became Reder's studio. Their major purchase was a block of stone over five feet long and nearly four feet square. From it Reder carved what is, by all odds, his finest sculpture in stone.

Wounded Woman (fig. 34) is related in concept to the Cuban tempera paintings, though obviously more compact and sculptural. The nude figure in the center is surrounded and supported by five

6. Two Birds. 1953.

Woodcut. 20 x 18.
World House Galleries.

other nude women whose massive bodies are twisted and turned in a variety of postures. Where formerly Reder had pierced the block in one or two places at most, he now cut multiple apertures from top and sides to its very core. The powerful rhythms of the supporting figures not only define the exterior of the stone; they also turn constantly inward toward its central axis, the recumbent woman. The relatively static balance of the earlier works has been replaced by a dynamic sequence of forms moving endlessly within the three-dimensional volume of the block. It is a work that demands to be seen from every conceivable approach, for each provides new interior vistas and new aspects of the complex flow of forms. Yet with all this involution and movement, it is a work of nearly classical poise, for every shape has its balance, every motion its counter. The skill with which this has been achieved within a three-dimensional space is a measure of Reder's stature as an artist.

Wounded Woman is also an incredible technical feat. The deep undercuttings, the carving of interior forms almost impossible to reach, with the attendant difficulties of seeing what one was doing or of having room to swing a hammer — all of these could hardly have been overcome without Reder's technical mastery and stubborness of spirit. As it was, the work nearly ended his career as a sculptor. For two years he labored at it. One day he was working on an inner area with his left arm thrust through a narrow opening holding the chisel, his right arm through another aperture holding the hammer. He tired but pushed himself on, as he had in the past. When he finally stopped and tried to withdraw his arms, he found he could not; the muscles refused to obey his command. For a long time he stood there imprisoned, like a man in the stocks. Eventually he dragged himself free by the weight of his body, but his arms hung useless at his sides. There followed seven months of partial paralysis before he was cured and able to start work on the *Wounded Woman* again. It took him another year to finish it, slightly over three and a half years in all.

It was not an easy time in Reder's life. A few woodcuts were sold, and a few private collectors bought sculpture — mostly small bronzes which he modeled while working on his big stone. The Whitney Museum represented him with six works in its exhibition of 1945, European Artists in America; Sturgis Ingersoll arranged to bring his surviving sculptures from Paris to New York after the war, as well as purchasing works for his own collection. But for seven years he had no dealer, almost no recognition and only sporadic sales. Small wonder that America seemed at times a hostile land, its indifference like a pillow that resumed its impenetrable mass after each small dent he made in it.

During his illness, when it was impossible to work on sculpture (except for one small bronze which he modeled with his left hand), Reder turned to drawings and woodcuts, as he had in France in 1940. Before that date he had done relatively few prints, and his drawings had been almost entirely figure studies related to his sculpture. But since that date his graphic work has become a major form of expression, quite apart from his carving or bronzes, though not entirely unrelated to the latter.

The freedom of graphic art, once it was pursued for its own sake, liberated Reder's imagination and stimulated a pictorial fantasy which had never found outlet in his carvings. His early subjects were drawn mostly from books, but the sources he chose are evidence of his bent:

7. Woman and Dog. 1956.

Ink. 25 ¼ x 18 ¼.
Whitney Museum of American Art.

8. The Balcony. 1956.

Ink. 19 x 26.
World House Galleries.

Rabelais, the Apocalypse, the life of Noah, Susanna and the Elders, the Song of Songs, the Seven Deadly Sins. Occasionally he made use of Jewish legends. *The Praying Rider* illustrates the tale of a poor water-carrier who was worshipping in the synagogue when he remembered that he had forgotten to water his own horse; whereupon he rode to the river in his prayer robes, scandalizing the community until the rabbi reminded them that one should do unto animals as one did unto men. But in recent years Reder has abandoned such subjects and depended solely on his own fertile imagination. He has invented a singular bestiary of strange birds and animals, sometimes vaguely recognizable as an owl, a bull, a cock, sometimes unlike anything on earth. His musical instruments are even odder: lutes with weirdly shaped sounding boxes and offset strings, horns with multiple apertures and a wilderness of keys and mouthpieces. In the costume of his women Reder has shown an extraordinary fecundity of invention. The variety of headdresses, veils, robes, capes, tiaras and diadems in which they are accoutered has a natural elegance never twice the same. While there is no narrative element in these later drawings and woodcuts, there is occasionally the hint of an enigmatic drama. *Monument in the Sea*, for instance, suggests the crumbling of an ancient civilization, while a number of drawings depicting plazas and balconied façades peopled by nude or heavily costumed women have the look of theatrical tableaux with an unexplained script. An aura of distant legend and fable fills these works, although Reder's imagination seems more concerned with the proliferation of unusual forms than with stories or explicit events.

Stylistically, the drawings vary widely. They are seldom done in pure line, for Reder loves the range of tone that broad washes contribute. These are often combined with linear passages of great delicacy, as in *Bride and Bull* (fig. 9) where the thin arabesques of the costume move like a shower of grace notes against the subtle tones of the background. Yet he can also draw with a brush in heavy, vigorous strokes which build up a dense network of black against the stark white of the paper, as in *Bust of a Man*. Between these poles, he has rung many variations.

The woodcuts have a different quality, which stems largely from the medium, although Reder uses it in a variety of unorthodox ways that widen its usual range of effects. He likes thin sheets of wood (often plywood) with enough grain to give variety to the solid areas. His design is sometimes gouged out deeply, sometimes barely scratched into the surface. The latter method gives him almost as much freedom as drawing and makes possible the complex swirls and flourishes of line that build up his fantastic forms. The final effect is achieved in the printing as much as in the cutting. The block is inked with extreme care; when different colors are used, they are applied to the various areas and are sometimes permitted to overlap each other. Where an opaque tone is wished colored ink is used, where a more brilliant or transparent tone is needed oil paint replaces it. The printing is always done by hand, and much of the tonal variation is achieved by altering the pressure in different areas. Only one impression is pulled from many of these blocks, for Reder's interest in the woodcut has nothing to do with its powers of multiplication. He loves the medium for its own sake — for the quality of line produced by the resistance of the wood to his tool, for the subtlety of tones achieved in the printing, for the softness of color absorbed into paper, for the grain and even the flaws in the surface of his blocks, which challenge him to turn them to aesthetic ends.

9. Bride and Bull. 1956.

Ink. 23¼ x 26½.
World House Galleries.

The fantasy, imagination and inventiveness of Reder's graphic work found almost no echo in his early sculpture, with its simple massive forms. *Wounded Woman*, however, began to point in a new direction, and in 1950, three years after it was finished, Reder completed several large stone pieces which are radically different from anything he had done before and closer in spirit to his drawings and woodcuts. *Bust of Centaur* (fig. 39) is a transparent head in which the features have been so freely distorted and dislocated that the work, at first sight, seems purely abstract. The nose is split into twin trunks, the ears curl forward like snakes, and a single sphere in the center serves for both eyeballs when seen through the apertures on opposite sides. *Fantastic Bird* (fig. 36) is even more grotesque, a hybrid creature, half human or animal in its anatomy, erupting in weird excrescences. Here, for the first time, Reder has not carved the stone into smooth, simple volumes but has left it rough and pitted, with many irregularities and tool marks. In both pieces the discipline of the block can still be felt, but the artist has pierced it and opened it to the ultimate extent that stone will permit. Except for a large unfinished *Two Centaurs*, these pieces, are the last carvings which he has done.

Reder turned to bronze "because it let my imagination grow." The technique he adopted was not the traditional one of modeling first in clay (a material he has disliked since the day it was forced on him at the Academy in Prague), but of working directly in plaster, built up over an armature. The process permits extreme freedom, and it released in Reder a torrent of imagery which has flowed unchecked ever since. During the four years that he remained in Forest Hills, he produced some fifteen major pieces in plaster, with such titles as *Woman with Bird, Lady with House of Cards, Noah's Wife Carrying Two Owls, Queen of the Amazons with Sceptre.* Unfortunately these larger works have not survived in their early versions. All that exists today from these years are a few smaller bronzes, but they are enough to show the freedom and extreme variety of Reder's work in the new medium. A prancing *Bull* (fig. 38) is extraordinarily free and energetic. A *Head of Noah* (fig. 43) looks like an explosion; the hair, the beard, even the features have been built out from the central mass in a heavy burst of form piled on form. In contrast, *La Belle Imperia* (fig. 41) introduces a tender and lyrical grace which is a new note in Reder's sculpture; the slender neck, the delicate features, the attenuated forms of the headdress make it one of his airiest pieces. Yet with all this freedom and openness of construction, it is apparent — as we shall see in greater detail later — that the memory of the block persists, that no motion is unrelated to a kind of aesthetic center of gravity about which the forms revolve and toward which they invariably return. As Reder puts it: "Give to stone what is for stone. Give to bronze what is for bronze. Both are in the block."

In 1948 Reder had become an American citizen. In 1951, the Grace Borgenicht Gallery became his dealer and gave him three one-man exhibitions at yearly intervals, although only one of these contained sculpture, and this was limited to smaller pieces. The Whitney Museum represented him in virtually all its sculpture Annuals from 1951 on, and his big *Wounded Woman* made a stir at the Fairmont Park Art Association's Third Sculpture International of 1949, where *Life* called it "the sensation of the show." The Museum of Modern Art acquired his stone *Torso* in 1953. While these successes were encouraging, Reder decided that he would like to live for a time in Italy where more people might believe in his work and where there were, in any case, better facilities for expert and inexpensive casting. In July 1954 the Reders closed the Forest Hills house, leaving behind them the plasters that were too big to transport, and set out for Europe.

The next four years were productive ones. The first two were spent in an apartment and workshop on the outskirts of Rome where Reder produced several large works in plaster — *The Conqueror, Woman with Bird, The Good Samaritan, Minotaur and Siren,* and many smaller pieces. All of these he was able to have cast in bronze at a foundry in Verona. In 1956 the Reders moved to Florence, partly to be nearer the foundry, but chiefly because they happened to meet the owner of the Palazzo Torrigiani, an elderly duke who rented them an apartment on the ground floor with four big rooms, a loggia and a private garden. Before he left Italy at the end of 1958, Reder had filled every corner of it with new bronzes, including second versions of several of the plasters left at Forest Hills.

One cannot easily separate the elements of Reder's art in the Italian bronzes. Fantasy of subject and formal inventiveness blend in-

10. Medieval Town. 1957.

Ink. 20 x 26.
World House Galleries.

extricably, for the exuberant fertility of the artist's imagination is at one with his baroque style. If Reder is asked, for instance, why *The Conqueror* (fig. 47) has four faces, he may reply, "Because I just don't like a face on only one side," or he may say that it was "an opportunity to make an all-around face," to render the piece equally interesting, in a formal sense, from every angle. And no doubt both reasons — the fantastic and the aesthetic — are equally true. Nor are they, for Reder, separate. "When art is infected by narration," he says, "then it is suspect." His fantasy is always formal rather than literary, even when it feeds on literary sources. *The Siticines with Falcon* (fig. 56) comes from Rabelais's account of Pantagruel's voyage to an island inhabited by beings half human, half bird, but for Reder, the subject became a visual challenge in the hybridization of form, the development of one species of form out of another. Many of the strange appurtenances in his sculpture, such as the stringed instrument in *Minotaur and Siren* (fig. 53), are there primarily for formal purposes — to close the composition, to carry the eye around and back to another volume, but this in no way lessens the play of imagination which has conceived so odd an object.

Sometimes Reder recalls the remote sources from which his concepts sprang; often he does not. The idea for *The Conqueror* came from a brightly colored statue of Napoleon which he bought as a youth in Czernowitz and kept for many years. *The Good Samaritan* (fig. 48) was based, as we have seen, on a childhood school composition. *Noah's Wife Carrying Two Owls* (fig. 70) is his tribute to the mother of all men, who is so singularly neglected in the Bible. The minotaurs, sirens and Amazons, which reappear often in his work, are obviously derived from Greek mythology, although it is significant that they never re-enact any specific myth. On the other hand, if Reder is asked why he conceived a *Flowering Cat* (fig. 46), he says, "I don't remember that. Perhaps it was because the cat is to me a proud sovereign and the flowering is an expression of her sovereignty. In any case, she didn't object." Nor can he tell now why (aside from formal reasons) a cow stands on a trapeze, a goat bears on its back a tremendous bell or a nude woman blows a trumpet that looks more like a huge flower than a musical instrument. All he can say of these is that they come, in some way, from Czernowitz with its rich springs of legend and folklore, of earthy humor and religious intensity. "We were born already drunk by fantasy."

If the sources of Reder's imagery are sometimes obscure, his development of the image, after its birth, is clearer. Certain things have plainly fascinated him — both for their formal possibilities and because they appeal to something in his heart or his imagination. These things he has used over and over in fresh combinations and variations. Animals, for instance, figure in many of his works, but only four of them: the horse, the goat, the cat, and the bull or cow. There are no dogs ("they are too slavish") and virtually no wild animals. There are, however, a few fishes and a great many birds; Reder has taken the latter through more formal variations than any of his other creatures, ranging from the identifiable owls on the shoulders of Noah's wife to the grotesque and nearly abstract fowl in *Woman with Bird* (fig. 42). And he has combined them with other creatures in imaginative compositions, such as his *Bird and Fishes* (fig. 58). He has played just as freely with the shapes of musical instruments, which abound in his work of this period and were to become even more prevalent after he left Italy. Trumpets are a favorite device, which he bends and twists into a variety of forms that often look organic rather than mechanical. Their repeated flaring bells play an important formal role in giving weight and motion to the upper part of *Bull Captured by the Amazons* (fig. 57) and at the same time contribute to its triumphant mood. The cello, in both the large and small versions of *Cello Player* (figs. 44, 60) has been transformed into a heavy, irregular mass, the bow into a club. It functions as a sculptural equivalent of the actual instrument and completes the circular, diagonal movement of the player; at the same time, its very heaviness suggests a deep sonority of tone. In the same way, *The Cymbal Player* (fig. 67) and *Tambourine* (fig. 68) are staccato compositions in which the nearly abstract shapes of the instruments play dual roles.

Among Reder's repertoire of forms and subjects, the female human body has always been paramount, but his treatment of it changed radically when he turned to bronze. A new sensuousness is apparent in the nudes. They are not the massive, block-like figures of his stone sculpture but more closely related to flesh and bone, more varied in proportion and structure. Some are slender and graceful,

11. The Angel. 1958.

Ink 25¾ x 19¾.
World House Galleries.

12. Girl. 1958.

Ink. 25¼ x 19½.
World House Galleries.

some are ripe and full-bodied, while in their freer actions there is often a sensuousness of attitude, as in *Trumpet Player Gargoyle* (fig. 61) or *Young Girl on a Tree* (fig. 71). An even greater change was Reder's increasing interest in the clothed figure and the great variety of things that could be done sculpturally with costume and head-dress. *La Belle Imperia* of 1953, while he was still in Forest Hills, was one of his first attempts to translate the complicated headgear which he had invented in his graphic work into sculptural terms. It was followed by a series of busts, such as *Head of Amazon with Diadem* (fig. 40), *Pallas Athena with Raven* (fig. 52), *Bust of Flower Girl* (fig. 45), in which the treatment of the hair and its trappings becomes increasingly ornate and imaginative as they combine in eruptions of nearly abstract form. In a small bronze of 1957, *The Cymbal Player* (fig. 67), he discovered that the entire costume could be made to suit a new sculptural purpose if parts of it were cut out in various patterns, opening vistas through the bronze to the forms beneath.

This device he carried even farther in the big *Lady with House of Cards* (fig. 69) of the same year. Here he flings the scarf out in an arching semicircle, but pierces it so that the back can be seen through it; at the same time he slashes the spreading skirt to reveal the solid column behind it. The dress thus becomes a kind of embroidery around the figure without ever totally concealing it, a counterpoint of complex shapes and movements against the relatively simple ones of the human body. The house of cards, too, functions as a transparent element through which the body is seen. In terms of design alone, the piece marks one more step in Reder's departure from solidity, his determination to lighten and open the volume of sculpture without destroying the volume itself. Several other single standing figures, such as *Woman with Bird* (fig. 42) or *The Huntress with Antelope in Cage* (fig. 76), show the same preoccupation. In both it is the objects carried that simultaneously open and complete the volume. The bird of the first piece is shaped like a reverse silhouette of the woman's body; the space between them is as important an element in the design as the solid forms themselves. The cage of the second piece and the looping coils of rope create a still more transparent play against the massive figure of the huntress.

To open volume and yet preserve it — to keep the sense of the block or sphere or column, the self-contained inviolate space, and yet to animate it to its very heart — this has been the ideal towards which Reder has worked since he first became a sculptor. The Italian bronzes as a whole represent his most dramatic step in this direction and a notable development of his ability to control and direct the most complex formal relations. It is the complexity of these pieces — their restless motion, eruption of detail and lively surfaces, often modeled to create a strong pattern of light and shade — that creates the baroque impression. It is the control, the discipline of the volume, that gives them their stability, their equilibrium, their essentially classical structure. The *Trumpet Player Gargoyle* (fig. 61) is a series of undulating forms and deeply shadowed recesses, yet it is also a complete sphere. *The Conquerer* (fig. 47) is a progression of contrasting forms and textures, from the sphere at its base to the rough escarpment of the cloak above, yet it has the strength and simplicity of a column. *Bull Captured by the Amazons* (fig. 57) is one of the most active pieces of them all; the multitude of arms, legs, spears and trumpets seem to writhe in continuous motion, but it is a consciously wrought design of circles moving within circles, all related to its controlling half-spherical form. In the same way, the heavy verticals and horizontals of *The Good Samaritan* (fig. 48) are related to the rectangular block. The only exceptions to this underlying geometry (if they can be called exceptions) are certain pieces, like *Noah's Wife Carrying Two Owls* (fig. 70), in which the true sculpture is contained in the upper part of the composition while the legs are, in Reder's words, "so to say, a pretext to keep the event up in the air." In this way he has been able to escape the limitations of a flat base and to create, from the hips up, a completely spherical composition.

What happens within Reder's encompassing volumes is equally important, for it is here that the animation takes place: the diagonals that cut suddenly across the curves, the counter motions and balances, the rhythms of forms repeated in variation, the correspondences of concave and convex. "When you see a sculpture your eye must have the possibility to walk up and down," Reder says, and he often conceives of the sequence of forms as "steps for the eye to walk on." It is a voyage interrupted, however, by many surprises, sudden obstacles thrown across the way like the raised pattern of the cards in *Lady with House of Cards*. At other times it is an aerial voyage as the eye is drawn across wide spaces by the recognition of echoing forms: the trumpets and trumpet-like headdresses of the Amazons or the peaked ears of the minotaur which are repeated in the horned projections of the musical instrument. Many of the formal relations are subtler. The heels, calves, thighs, buttocks and breasts of the *Trumpet Player Gargoyle* form a sequence of round bosses which have their counter in the concavity of the trumpet. The curve of the beast's neck in *Minatour and Siren* (fig. 53) is balanced precisely by the curve of the woman's helmet, and both are related to the curves of her left arm and bent leg; together they carry the eye around the whole piece in a graceful sweep, making it one of Reder's most satisfying circular compositions. One could take a similar journey through all his bronzes and find that, while the basic means and the basic sculptural concepts are the same, the variety of forms and the inexhaustible freshness of invention make each a new experience.

In Florence, Reder began to be known. The Galleria d'Arte Moderna L'Indiano gave an exhibition of his graphic work in 1956; a year later, on the occasion of his sixtieth birthday, it exhibited twelve of his bronzes while eighteen more were put on public display in the rooms and garden of the Palazzo Torrigiani where the Reders lived. The Italian critics gave his work several long and laudatory reviews. John Rewald's monograph was published in Florence the same year.

But Florence was not a city of collectors, and despite the pleasures of life there, it soon became apparent that the sculpture now crowding their loggia and garden must find its way to an adequate exhibition in New York. In April, 1958, World House Galleries offered to become his dealer and he accepted. A one-man exhibition was planned for late January, 1959. The preceding fall, Reder shipped some two dozen bronzes to the gallery. In December he and his wife followed them to New York, where they took a studio on East 75th Street and an apartment next door.

The World House exhibition brought a selection of Reder's major sculpture to the public for the first time in this country, and resulted, directly or indirectly, in a wider recognition than he had yet received. The Whitney Museum showed his *Noah's Wife Carrying Two Owls* in its sculpture Annual and later purchased his *Adam and Eve* (fig. 65). The Museum of Modern Art acquired his *Lady with House of Cards*. The one dark cloud was the illness of his wife, which hospitalized her for several months late in 1959. It was then that he created *Aaron with Tabernacle* (fig. 80), his starkest and most majestic bronze, quite unlike the others with their joyful sensuousness. "I knew that I have to create a center of discipline and morale, and I have to bring her every day to the hospital news about this center — positive news. I chose Aaron because it was he who kept the Jews together when Moses was on Mount Sinai."

Fortunately his wife recovered. Early in 1960, Reder won a Ford Foundation grant of ten thousand dollars, one of ten artists selected by an eminent jury for this honor. In May the Reders went to Florence for two weeks to close the apartment there and ship the remaining bronzes to New York. The rest of the summer they spent at Verona where Reder practically lived at the foundry, casting the plasters which had been left at Florence and the new ones done in New York. He also found time to create seven pieces directly in wax at the foundry. They returned to New York in the fall of 1960.

13. Woman on Horse. 1959.

Ink. 28¼ x 33.
World House Galleries.

In the two and one half years that he has occupied the New York studio, Reder has worked harder than at any time in his life. He has produced an astonishing volume of sculpture, from dozens of small pieces to five huge ones, all over six feet high. He has also done a quantity of graphic work. And, returning to a field that has long fascinated him, he has spent months at a time working exclusively on architectural projects, several of which he had conceived in Czernowitz some thirty years before.

14. Woman with Blue Hat. 1961.

Woodcut. 23¼ x 21.
World House Galleries.

Reder's interest in architecture grew initially from his concern with the proper display of sculpture as a three-dimensional art, although it has since ranged far beyond that problem. It will be recalled that early in his career he had designed a circular exhibition building in which the pieces acted as caryatids. This, he now felt, had two disadvantages: it was inflexible as a museum, and it still did not escape sufficiently from the traditional approach at a single level across a flat floor. The problem, as he saw it, was to destroy the horizontal view, or rather to make it one of many, so that all the relations of sculptural volumes could be seen from every conceivable side and angle. The floor, therefore, must go, and also the traditional vertical walls which so often obscured one or more aspects of a piece. "It is an utter contradition," he wrote, "that a spatial art like sculpture should be kept subjugated to non-spatial traditions." The highly original solution which he finally devised (fig. 17) was a building based on the structure of the honeycomb, capable of infinite expansion by the addition of new "cells." In each unit of this structure, the floor, ceiling and walls have been reduced to a minimum. The spectator moves freely in three dimensions, back and forth, up and down, on stairs which mount the sloping sides or on ramps which circle at different elevations within the unit. Inside this open space, unbroken by walls or partitions, the sculpture can be displayed at a great variety of levels. Simple platforms, adjusted to the steps and the slope of the sides, provide movable bases that can be installed temporarily at virtually any point. The effect, to judge from Reder's model, is not unlike being inside a giant, light-filled crystal.

From the exhibition building (which he also conceives as the basic design for a sculptor's studio) Reder has branched out into other equally unorthodox and imaginative projects. The search for an atmosphere of spiritual harmony marks all of these. "Human love is basic to being a good architect," he says. Human love translated into architectural terms means, for Reder, three things: space in which to move freely, lightness of weight, an equilibrium between the horizontal and the vertical. He dislikes crowds or crowding and is convinced that many of the complexes of modern society are produced by tall buildings and by physically heavy buildings which weigh upon the spirit. Nothing he has designed is higher than its length. "Verticality makes people afraid; too much horizontality is boring." Structurally, his buildings are conceived in terms of thin steel, plastics and the new synthetic building materials of the greatest lightness and strength. He is not, however, a trained architect or an engineer, and he was delighted to discover that Buckminster Fuller had already devised and tested a system of construction that accorded perfectly with many of his own ideas. James W. Fitzgibbon and C. David Sides, Jr., of Fuller's firm, Synergetics, have been equally interested in Reder's designs and have produced the models and structural drawings for several of them. The architect, I. M. Pei, has also followed his work with interest.

To Reder the sphere is the most satisfactory sculptural form because it is a perfectly unified and uniform volume with no front or back, no top or bottom, no frontality. He has used it in one of his most unusual architectural projects, a theater conceived entirely in the round (fig. 26). The stage, with transparent floor and transparent sets, is suspended in the center. A single row of seats moves on a spiral track around the interior walls, climbing slowly to the apex of the globe, then turning and descending on a parallel track. A stationary ramp behind the seats provides access. During the course of a performance, each spectator would view the stage from every side and from every conceivable angle. He would see the actors from below, through the transparent floor; later he would look down on the tops of their heads. The performance thus becomes a kind of mobile sculpture that must always be conceived and executed in the round. Like the exhibition building, this project is closely linked to Reder's "volumetric" aesthetic. It also illustrates his concern for the inhabitants of his buildings (nobody takes a back seat) and his love of uncrowded space (maximum capacity is 180, "and that already is a crowd").

It is perhaps significant that both the exihibition building and the theater were conceived in Czernowitz at a time when Reder was carving stone; they have the simple geometrical volumes and the compactness of his early sculpture. The later architectural projects seem more closely related to his bronzes; they are more open in design, more varied in shape, and are composed of many separate elements connected by ramps, exterior walks, bridges, and the like. The living room of his one-family pavilion (fig. 20), for instance, is formed like an inverted boat, and this arched shape is repeated with variations in the smaller wings which provide the bed rooms and other functional quarters, most of them circled by an elaborate system of balconies. Beneath the living room the same arched shape extends downward to create a swimming pool. It is in domestic architecture that Reder feels the most imperative psychological need for lightness of construction. His house seems to float in the air, supported by slender arcs of stainless steel. Its walls (not one of them vertical or flat) are made entirely of a tinted transparent plastic which can be made opaque, for privacy, by an electrical charge. The entire building would weigh some 20,000 pounds, and this extreme lightness would have practical as well as spiritual advantages. His houses could, he believes, be fabricated at a central point and flown by helicopter to distant sites; by the same means a family could take its house with it when it moved, or even use it in different locations in summer and winter. Whether or not this vision could ever be fulfilled, the one-family pavilion is, in terms of living, supremely airy and spacious — an environment, as he says, "for human love."

Reder's plan for a coastal town called Gutzala (fig. 24) carries still further his concept of open design within a unified whole. It was first inspired by the crowded conditions of Venice, but he likes to envisage it as rising somewhere along the California coast. Basically it is a circle, though quite irregular in form. At the center, a cluster of islands contains a theater, a town hall and other public buildings. Private dwellings encircle the central complex on more remote islands and along the coastal strip of the mainland. At the seaward extreme are breakwaters, and inside them a huge geodesic dome, built on Buckminster Fuller principles, is supported, umbrella-like, over the water to shelter aquatic festivals and other public events. The stores and other facilities are inland. An elevated highway, with a system of ramps and walks, is threaded through the buildings on shore, but the islands are accessible only by boat. It is the water, more than anything, that gives the city its character and unity. Unlike Venice, there are no narrow, winding canals, no press of buildings to hide the shining expanse of sea. The entire plan is comprehensible from any point except the business section (which Reder has not even bothered to include in his model). This combination of

15. Boy with Palette. 1961.

Woodcut. 25½ x 22.
World House Galleries.

unity and space could scarcely be realized in a city of any size; Reder's is more truly a small town. But a dispersion of population is part of his program. Cities like New York are to him a nightmare of crowds, heavy masonry and frightening verticality. He looks to a day when they will be abandoned for all except commercial purposes, when men will live in rationally conceived communities, human in scale, united by a plan which is, itself, an expression of human love.

There is nothing abstract in Reder's architectural concepts. They are born of his own physical and spiritual needs, and no technical obstacle daunts him in seeking a solution to these. When he went to Europe in the spring of 1960 he was so oppressed by his windowless inside stateroom that he undertook, a few months later, the design of an ocean liner (fig. 25) in which every room would have natural light and air. He achieved this by abandoning the traditional monolithic superstructure and replacing it with eleven elevated pavilions built of light synthetic materials and supported by stainless steel. The concept is not unlike that of his coastal city, the public rooms forming a nucleus around which the living quarters are dispersed in an open plan that provides even the crew's quarters with pleasant vistas. At first he paid no more attention to the hull than he had to the shopping center of his town; it would be a conventional one housing the machinery and cargo. Then he heard by chance of experiments with hydrofoils (wing-like projections which permit a vessel to plane over the surface instead of forcing its way through

17. Model of Exhibition Building for Volumetric Sculpture with Volumetric Approach. 1959.

Collection of the artist.

16. Drawing of Model of Exhibition Building for Volumetric Sculpture with Volumetric Approach. 1959.

By Synergetics, Inc. Project architect, C. David Sides, Jr.
Collection of the artist.

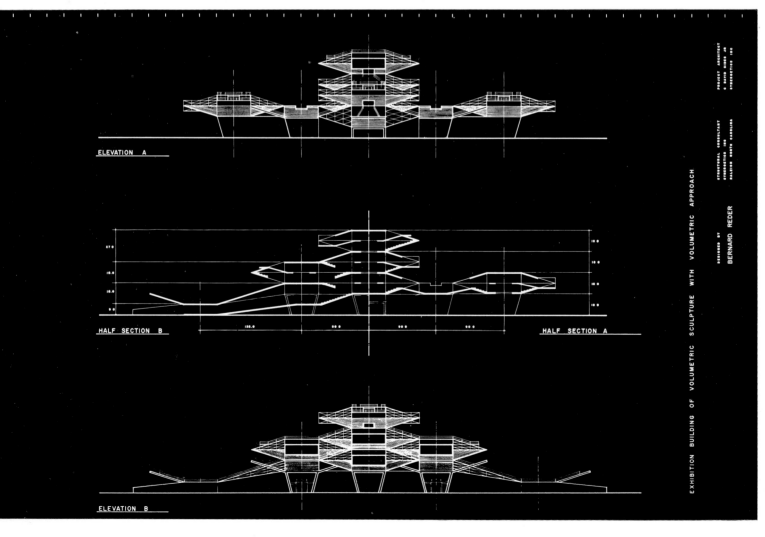

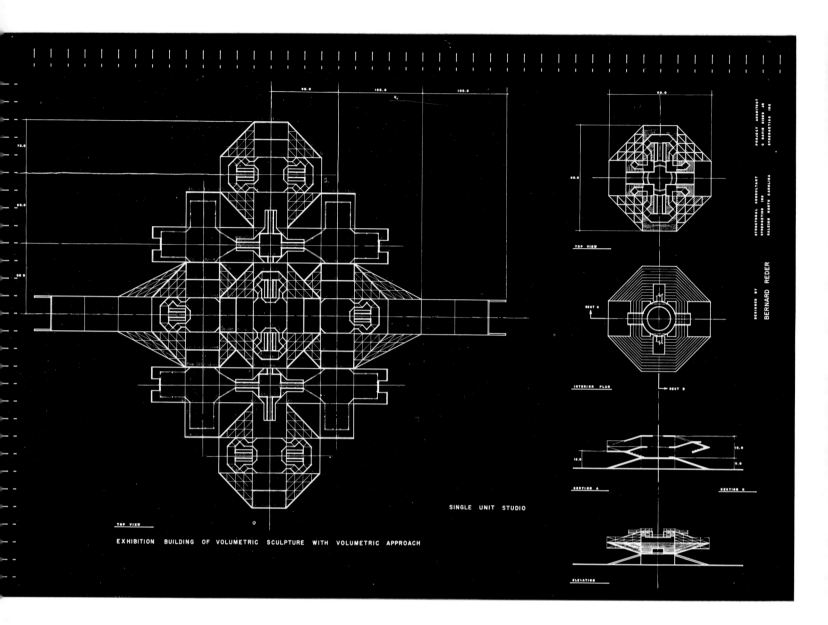

TOP VIEW

EXHIBITION BUILDING OF VOLUMETRIC SCULPTURE WITH VOLUMETRIC APPROACH

SINGLE UNIT STUDIO

TOP VIEW

INTERIOR PLAN

ELEVATION

BERNARD REDER

18. Drawing of Model of Exhibition Building for Volumetric Sculpture with Volumetric Approach.

1959.

By Synergetics, Inc. Project architect, C. David Sides, Jr.
Collection of the artist.

the water) and realized that the relative lightness of his own ship would lend itself well to this method of propulsion. So the *Ghitala* — named for his wife — is now a hydrofoil craft, although he is still content to leave technical details to the naval architects.

The twenty months from January 1959 (when he first moved into his New York studio) to September 1960 (when he temporarily stopped work on sculpture to prepare for his exhibition at the Whitney Museum) were also the most productive in Reder's entire career as a sculptor. During this brief period he created and cast some two dozen bronzes, of which at least ten were major pieces running from three to eight feet in height. The richness of imagery, the variety and formal inventiveness of these late bronzes is no less astonishing than the speed with which they were produced. It is almost as if they sprang from Reder's mind without the hindrance of technical procedures, and indeed his handling of plaster has become so assured that the array of tools he once used is now largely discarded. "It is curious," he remarks, "as an artist grows older the less tools he needs: I have come to a point where I use one spatula, one rasp." All the recent plasters were done with this simplicity of means.

Of the new pieces, the big *Aaron with Tabernacle* (fig. 80) stands somewhat apart, more austere and monumental than most of Reder's

19. Model of Modular Unit of Exhibition Building Used as a Studio. 1959.

Collection of the artist.

work. The subject appears to have come from the opening sentence of the *Book of Numbers:* "And on the day that the tabernacle was reared up the cloud covered the tabernacle, namely, the tent of the testimony: and at even there was upon the tabernacle as it were the appearance of fire, until the morning." Here is the tabernacle, the fire, the surrounding tents of the Israelites, but as usual the concept is more imaginative than illustrative. Aaron has become a giant, cradling an entire landscape in his arms. Nowhere is Reder's brilliant use of scale more apparent than in the tremendous hands which give the figure so much of its majesty without, miraculously, the appearance of distortion. Formally, the piece is a culmination of those single standing figures carrying objects, such as the *Lady with House of Cards* or *The Huntress with Antelope in Cage*, but it goes beyond any of them in complex, open organization. The robes flow out, tier upon tier, the outer ones completely separated from the body and affording vistas that pierce the solidity of the trunk. The fingers, the columns and tents, the peaked cap form a blocky forest of rising verticals countered by the descending sleeves and the horns which project downward from the periphery of the landscape. "Without those horns going down," says Reder, "the fingers would become narrative." Perhaps the key motif of the piece is the device which tops the tabernacle. This is a three-dimensional equivalent of a Hebrew letter which is one of God's initials. It is not only vital to the design, balancing the head of Aaron and offsetting the pyramid of the tabernacle with its own inverted pyramid, but it also establishes the dominant block-like forms of the piece, or at least of its upper cube, for this is another work where "the main event" is up in the air. Its use has more than a religious significance for Reder, who has always felt a deep affinity between the sculptural quality of the Hebrew alphabet and his own work.

At a nearly opposite pole is the *Bride and Bull* (fig. 81), another major piece done in 1959. Here the mood is gentle, the forms simpler and more clearly related to the block. The subject is entirely imaginary. Not until it was finished did Reder hear that in Andalusia the bride customarily accompanied the groom on a mule or other animal to get the marriage license. While the headdress is based on the traditional Jewish huppah, it, too, is primarily a product of Reder's

20. Model of One-Family Pavilion, I. 1959.

Collection of the artist.

imagination; in it he has combined the pierced pattern of *The Cymbal Player* with the raised pattern of the house of cards to create a sculptural motif that is both transparent and animated. His bull, meek and devoted, is in striking contrast to the usual concept of the animal.

Woman with Sphere and Pyramid (fig. 85), a third major piece of 1959, illuminates still another aspect of Reder's work. It is built almost entirely of geometrical shapes, for the skirt and cloak echo the pyramid while the head and breasts are almost as circular as the sphere. The subject itself has no significance aside from a formal one; it was consciously devised by Reder to demonstrate that a virtually abstract composition could be built with natural, unfragmented forms. "I could not resist to give by this theme my reaction against abstraction — to say it is not necessary to break things." Like many of Reder's works, the piece exists in more than a single version; a small one of 1958 demonstrates both the inception of the idea and how much further he carried the geometry in the later version by clothing the woman and reducing in relative size the bush or tree that breaks the smooth face of the pyramid (fig. 77).

A similar development of forms and themes through several variations — some minor, some major — can be found in much of Reder's recent work. Frequently he makes more than one cast of a piece, but they are never identical. There are three of *Flowering Cat*, for instance, with the flowers disposed differently in each; there are two of *Lady with House of Cards*, but the arm supporting the house is higher in one than in the other, and the angle of the card held aloft has been altered. Sometimes Reder will use older devices or even actual pieces in new combinations. The house of cards appears in two smaller and later bronzes, *Bird with House of Cards* and *Nude*

21. Drawing of Model of
One-Family Pavilion, I. 1959.

By Synergetics, Inc.
Project architect,
C. David Sides, Jr.
Collection of the artist.

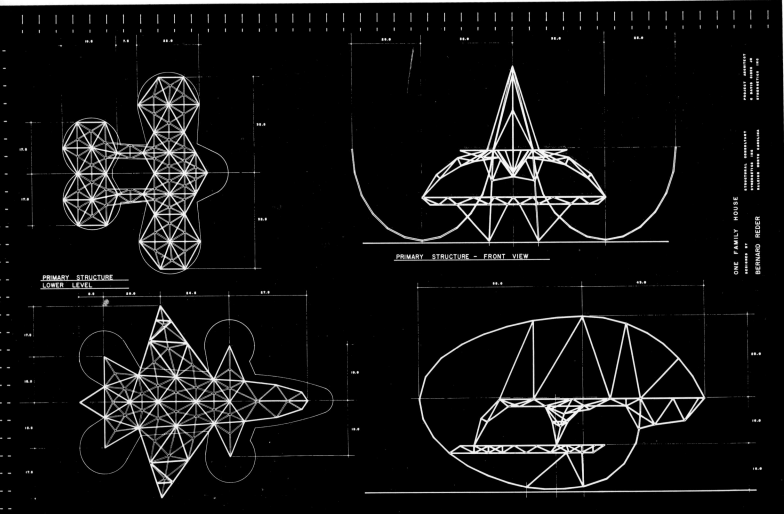

PRIMARY STRUCTURE
LOWER LEVEL

PRIMARY STRUCTURE - FRONT VIEW

PRIMARY STRUCTURE - UPPER LEVEL

PRIMARY STRUCTURE - SIDE VIEW

ONE FAMILY HOUSE

BERNARD REDER

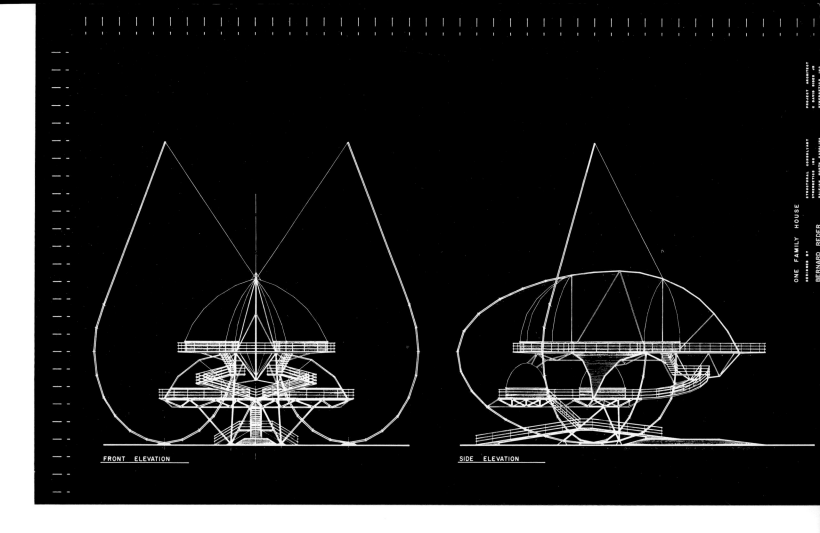

FRONT ELEVATION

SIDE ELEVATION

ONE FAMILY HOUSE

DESIGNED BY

BERNARD REDER

PROJECT ARCHITECT
C DAVID SIDES JR

22. Drawing of Model of One-Family Pavilion, I. 1959.

By Synergetics, Inc.
Project architect,
C. David Sides, Jr.

with House of Cards (fig. 79), entirely different from each other and from the large piece, while *La Gargouillade* (fig. 88), cast in 1960, assembles several trumpet-playing figures, done in Italy three or four years before, on a tree-like shaft which Reder created at the foundry in order to unite them. And this solution, in turn, was suggested by a still older composition, *Trumpet Tree*, in which he had built a similar cluster of forms on a central trunk.

A certain logic of imagination, coupled with an inherent dislike of uniformity, seems to lie behind this theme-and-variation aspect of Reder's work. His formal discoveries are seldom exhausted in a single piece, but are never repeated without assuming a new character. A kind of chain reaction is set up as certain pieces suggest multiple new approaches, and these, as they are explored, often turn out to be as fruitful as their parents. While some works, like *Bride and Bull*, have not yet produced offspring, the majority of Reder's bronzes belong to several thematic lines of development, which are never entirely separate and blend at various points. The single figure carrying an object, the women in trees, the fruit vendors and trumpet players are some of the older and longer lines that may still continue into the future.

Two new lines have also appeared since 1959. One consists of the piano and organ players, and is, so far, limited to small pieces. In these a woman sits at her instrument in the characteristic pose of playing. The sinuous curve of the grand piano with the lid raised has always appealed to Reder, and in treating it sculpturally (fig. 94) he has compressed and strengthened it and carried something of the same curve through the lines of the player's body. In the organ he has found an even greater challenge and a greater opportunity for imaginative variations (figs. 83, 89). Sometimes the pipes look like

23. Model of One-Family Pavilion,
II. 1959.

Collection of the artist.

flowers or trumpets, sometimes like the upstretched necks of young birds singing, while the keys have been magnified into blocks and arranged in free patterns only remotely related to the disposition of the manuals. Moreover, the organ lends itself admirably to Reder's concept of bronze sculpture as a block opened to the utmost transparency; the pipes define the limit of the volume, and the space between them creates constantly changing views to the interior of the piece.

The other recent series might be called women-with-multiple-tubular-instruments. The instruments are a bagpipe, an improbable trumpet with a single mouthpiece and seven horns, and an equally fantastic telescope with a single eyepiece and eight barrels. Although the works differ considerably and range from the relatively naturalistic *Bagpipe Player* (fig. 84) to the highly attenuated *Woman Astronomer I* and *II* (fig. 97), it is apparent that Reder's interest is the same in all. Basically he is working with a more completely open volume than he had ever attempted before, a volume animated by forms that radiate from a point at its center like a star or a contained explosion. This is particularly evident in the two *Woman Astronomers*, spherical compositions (established by the curve of the eyepiece and the woman's body) through which the legs and tubes of the instrument spread outward at varying angles. The stool is a second and quieter radiation of lines within the same space.

When Reder was in Verona during the summer of 1960 to cast

his most recent plasters, he began to explore a technique he had not used before — that of working directly in wax at the foundry so that the pieces could be cast immediately (by the lost-wax process) without the various intermediate steps required when the work was done first in plaster. The method is one of great spontaneity and requires a sure knowledge of intentions. Two kinds of wax are used: a hard wax in sheets, which must be warmed until flexible, then shaped and applied to the piece with a hot iron before it becomes cool and brittle again; also a soft wax, which is easily modeled and never hardens but can be employed only for details (like a nose) where its weight will not pull it out of shape. No armature is needed for smaller works, and the technique has generally been limited to these. It is possible, however, to use light sugar canes as a kind of armature, built into the piece as the work progresses to support extended forms and larger volumes. With their aid, Reder performed some extraordinary feats with wax on a bigger scale than is usually attempted.

Reder took to this technique as if it had been invented expressly for his purposes; he produced no less than seven pieces in the last few weeks of his stay at Verona. "Artistic spontaneity is today only completely possible in wax," he says. And just as his evolution from stone to plaster had released new forms and a new imagery, so — to a lesser degree — did the wax. The qualities of the material appealed to him. "The wax itself feels so good in my hands that I trust it to tell me what it wants; wax has special wishes." The new iconography and forms that resulted are, as usual, inseparable. *Seated Dwarf with Cat's Cradle* (fig. 92) demonstrates this more clearly perhaps than

24. Model of the Coastal Town, *Gutzala*. 1960.

Collection of the artist.

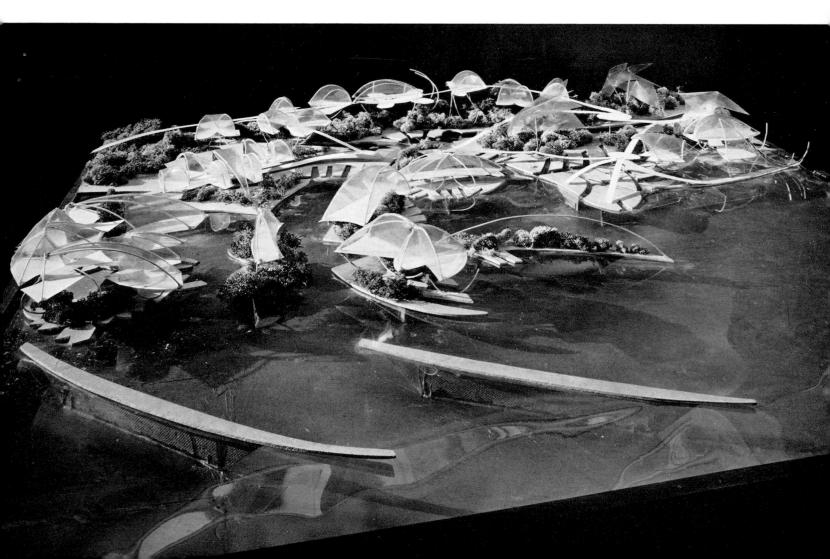

25. Model of the Boat, *Ghitala*. 1960.
   Collection of the artist.

any other piece. "I wanted very often to make a big head," Reder explains. "But I was reluctant. I am so deeply rooted in nature that I always retired from this idea. Suddenly one day I remembered this dwarf in Czernowitz with a big head, so I thought now it will be done. Then I decided I wanted him to have outstretched arms and fingers. But there must be a reason, so I thought of the cat's cradle. Sometimes the form brings out the reason, sometimes the reason brings out the form. And to find out which came first I do not care."

In these latest bronzes, Reder has utilized the wax for effects which would have been difficult to achieve in plaster. The clothing of the *Seated Dwarf with Cat's Cradle* has a thinness and fluidity which was plainly the result of bending single sheets into the required forms. Since the wax is light and strong enough to support its own weight when cool, such forms need no attachment at their edges; they can float in space. They can also be snipped into free-standing patterns, as he has done with the crab's claws in *Dwarf and Crab* (fig. 86). When the wax sheets are formed into enclosed volumes, like the skirt in the same piece, something else happens which is again different from plaster. The several sheets used meet at angles, and the lines of their juncture remain (intentionally) quite apparent in the finished work. The result is a blockier, more geometrical form, which Reder often uses as an extreme contrast to the free patterns of the open shapes.

26. Drawing of Model of Theater in a Sphere. 1927/61.

By Synergetics, Inc. Project architect, C. David Sides, Jr.
Collection of the artist.

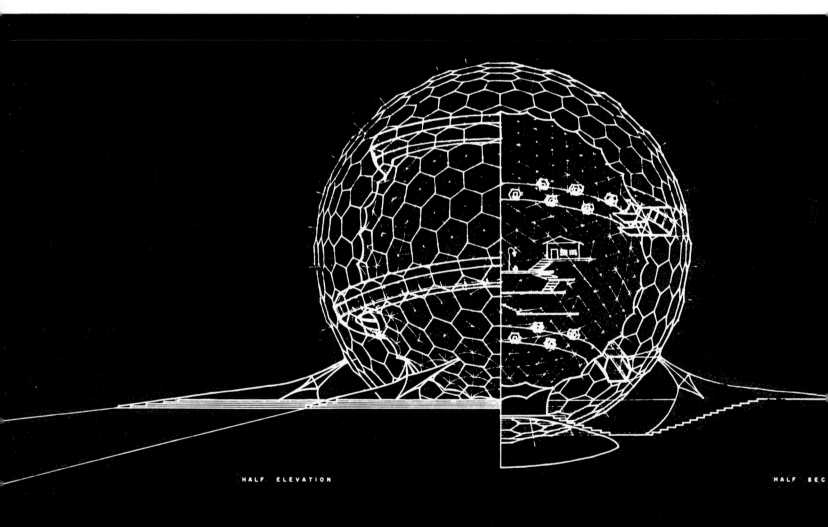

HALF ELEVATION

HALF SEC

A THEATER IN A SPHERE
CONCEPT BY BERNARD REDER

All of these points of difference between plaster and wax can be seen most clearly by comparing the two *Harp Players,* the first version (fig. 90) done in plaster, the second (fig. 91) entirely in wax. The former, when it was first executed, seemed Reder's most daring penetration of the block, its heavy forms projected into space with only the most tenuous connection to the base. But the second goes much farther, and is richer, too, in the variety of its forms. Here the points of attachment between harp and woman are so slight that the figure appears truly airborn. Its lightness is emphasized by the thinness of the sleeves with their deep concavities, while the hands have been freed to create a counterpoint of star-like radiations. When one realizes that this piece is seven feet high — nearly twice the height of the first — one can only marvel at the technical skill which Reder achieved in the new medium within so short a span of time.

Although the *Harp Player* was conceived in New York and belongs to a long sequence of musical themes, the majority of the pieces done in wax are new subjects and among the most fantastic that Reder's fertile imagination has produced. The spontaneity with which he was working appears to have stimulated recollections of Czernowitz (such as the dwarf who appears in two of these pieces) and to have suggested sculptural means of expressing them. The watchmaker-philosopher with a perverse penchant for reversing things was another figure from childhood who came to mind. Reder recalled his dissertations on the Jewish proverb, "Each man possesses his own quirk," which he maintained should be, "Each quirk possesses its own man." The sculpture of the latter title (fig. 87) combines a fantastically garbed figure with a hybrid creature, half bird, half animal. Seldom has Reder taken such liberties with anatomy. The man's hands are as claw-like as the beast's, his torso is a cylinder, his head has been elongated until it is nearly as long as the strange cap. The lightest of contacts joins the two figures, and this delicacy, combined with the bold and arbitrary shapes, has, as always, a dual function: it holds the spherical design together with a spring-like tension, and it creates much of the fairy-tale mood of the piece.

But Czernowitz was not the only source for these bronzes. Pure fantasy produced the *Snake and Crab* (fig. 96) with its playful contrast of sinuous and ragged forms, its Aesopian atmosphere. An 18th-century print in a dental office was the unprecedented starting point of another. This depicted, according to its legend, the balloon ascension of Tessu-Brissy at Limoges in 1786, and portrayed a dignified man on horseback in the wicker gondola of his aircraft, staring placidly over the landscape below. It so delighted Reder that he persuaded the dentist to exchange it for one of his own woodcuts. Needless to say, the scene was radically transformed when it became sculpture, the proportions altered and the whole design compressed into a single volume. Nevertheless, it still maintains some of the bland eccentricity of the original.

One of the last pieces which Reder completed at Verona in 1960 is perhaps the most impressive, so far, of his whole career. This is the big and incredibly complex *Two Women in the Jungle* (fig. 95), over six feet high and nearly five feet in diameter. In Florence, three years earlier, he had done a small version of the same subject, *Two Women on a Tree* (fig. 72). He had also started the large work but had been forced to leave it unfinished when he came to New

28. Torso, II. 1930.

Czech sandstone. 43 high.
World House Galleries.

27. Crouching Woman. 1930.

Czech sandstone. 26 high.
World House Galleries.

29. Two Bathers. 1934.

Pewter. 12 high.
Collection of Mr. and Mrs. Joseph D. Isaacson.

30. Bather. 1934.

Bronze. 18 long.
World House Galleries.

31. Bather, I. 1933.

Czech sandstone. 52½ long.
Collection of Jay C. Leff.

32. Two Seated Women. 1934.

Bronze. 10 long.
Collection of Mr. and Mrs. Rudolph J. Boyko.

33. Torso. 1939.

French limestone. 45 high.
The Museum of Modern Art.
Gift of J. van Straaten.

34. Wounded Woman. 1943-47.

Italian limestone. 62 long.
World House Galleries.

36. Fantastic Bird. 1950.

Alabama limestone. 48 high.
World House Galleries.

37. Europa and
    Bull. 1949.

    Bronze. 13½ long.
    Collection of Mr.
    and Mrs. Raphael
    H. Rhodes

38. Bull. 1953.

    Collection of Mr.
    and Mrs. Raphael
    H. Rhodes.

39. Bust of
Centaur. 1950.

Alabama limestone.
39½ high.
World House
Galleries.

40. Head of Amazon with Diadem. 1954.

Bronze. 23 high.
World House Galleries.

41. La Belle Imperia. 1953.

Bronze. 18 high.
Collection of Mr. and Mrs. Phillip A.
Bruno.

42. Woman with
    Bird. 1954.

Bronze. 77 high.
World House
Galleries.

43. Head of Noah. 1954.
Bronze. 20½ high.
Collection of Mr. and Mrs. Raphael H. Rhodes.

44. Cello Player, I. 1955.
Bronze. 16 high.
Joseph H. Hirshhorn Collection.

45. Bust of Flower Girl. 1955.

Bronze. 26¾ high.
World House Galleries.

46. Flowering Cat. 1955.

Bronze. 27 long.
Collection of Mrs. Gertrud A. Mellon.

47. The Conqueror. 1955.

Bronze. 69 high.
World House Galleries.

48. The Good Samaritan. 1955.

Bronze. 41 high.
World House Galleries.

49. Hasid with Bird. 1955.

Bronze. 25¼ high.
Collection of Dr. Morton Hecht, Jr.

50. Head of the Good Samaritan. 1955.

Bronze. 9¼ high.
Collection of Mr. and Mrs. Jacob Hacken.

51. Head of Siren. 1955.

Bronze. 19 high.
Collection of Mrs. Gertrud A. Mellon.

52. Pallas Athena with Raven. 1955.

Bronze. 28½ high.
World House Galleries.

53. Minotaur and Siren. 1955.

Bronze. 59 high.
World House Galleries.

54. Lady and Fruit. 1955.

Bronze. 15½ long.
Collection of Mr. and Mrs. John Rewald.

55. Playing Fish. 1955.

Bronze. 30 high.
World House Galleries.

56. The Siticines with Falcon. 1955.

Bronze. 62 high.
World House Galleries.

57. Bull Captured by the Amazons. 1956.
Bronze. 48 high.
Collection of Mr. and Mrs. William P. Wood.

58. Bird and Fishes. 1956.

Bronze. 25½ high.
World House Galleries.

59. Triumphant Amazons. 1956.

Bronze. 24½ high.
Collection of Mr. and Mrs. R. Sturgis Ingersoll.

60. Cello Player, II. 1956.

Bronze. 51 high.
World House Galleries.

61. Trumpet Player Gargoyle. 1956.

Bronze. 39½ high.
World House Galleries.

62. Goat Carrying the Bell. 1956.

Bronze. 52 high.
World House Galleries.